AGAINST
DREAMING

Other Books by C. G. Hanzlicek

POETRY

Living in It 1971

Stars 1977

Calling the Dead 1982

A Dozen for Leah 1982

When There Are No Secrets 1986

Mahler: Poems and Etchings 1993

TRANSLATIONS

*A Bird's Companion:
American Indian Songs* 1974

*Mirroring: Selected Poems of
Vladimir Holan* 1985

AGAINST DREAMING

Poems by
C. G. Hanzlicek

University of Missouri Press
Columbia and London

Copyright © 1994 by C. G. Hanzlicek
University of Missouri Press, Columbia, Missouri 65201
Printed and bound in the United States of America
All rights reserved
5 4 3 2 1   98 97 96 95 94

Library of Congress Cataloging-in-Publication Data

Hanzlicek, C. G., 1942-
    Against dreaming : poems / by C. G. Hanzlicek.
      p. cm.
    ISBN 0–8262–0932–7 (cloth : alk. paper). —ISBN 0-8262-0933-5
    (pbk. : alk. paper)
    I. Title.
    PS3558.A544A7   1994
    811'.54—dc20

                                         93-33656
                                           CIP

Designer and Typesetter: Kristie Lee
Printer and Binder: Thomson-Shore, Inc.
Typeface: Palatino, Astaire and Futuri Condensed

    The author wishes to thank the editors of the following journals, in which
some of these poems originally appeared: *Antioch Review, Arete: Forum for
Thought, The Bloomsbury Review, Caprice, The Kenyon Review, The New England
Review-Middlebury Series, The Midnight Lamp, Poetry, Poetry Northwest,* and *South
Florida Poetry Review.*
    "Egg," and "Against Dreaming" were anthologized in *Piecework,* Silver Skates
Publishing, 1987. "Cemetery in Dolni Dobrouc, Czechoslovakia," "Prague
Wreaths," and "Prague, Late November, 1989," appeared in *The Boundaries of
Twilight: A Collection of Czechoslovak-American Writing,* New Rivers Press, 1991.
"Night Game" first appeared as a chapbook printed by Michael Peich at Aralia
Press. The nine Mahler poems, with accompanying etchings by Olda Prochazka
were first published in a limited edition by Brighton Press in 1993. My special
thanks to Bill Kelly and Michele Burgess for such a lovely book.

for Peter Everwine

Contents

THIS LIFE

CZECHOSLOVAKIA

MAHLER

THIS LIFE

Men at Forty-Five

Are half-dead,
And they know,
When the light is right,
When the mirror is a highly polished blade,
Even that is a wildly optimistic nod
Unearned by their habits.
The habits, fought for against those who love them,
Against common sense, too,
Will die as hard as they will,
And the sermons thrown at them
Are foreknown;
Why preach to these soon to be old
Priests of whole wheat bread,
Trout, alfalfa sprouts?
They look in the mirror
And are overtaken by a most natural
Question: could it be that face
Has given more than it's taken?
If only each dietary discretion
Led to the pleasures of an indiscretion . . .
If only one could expand, not contract . . .
Do you see what they face
In their faces?
There is all the time in the world
For misery;
It's the world's specialty,
But one little pleasure,
One little nick
On the edge of the blade of time,
Seems harder and harder to come by.
And the mirror of morning

Is only meant to shave in.
Death will hold up a mirror
We are meant to measure our lives in.
Wish us well,
Wish well the men of forty-five,
Who can no longer deny
The imponderable size of that mirror,
The size of their lives,
And want to shrink the one
And magnify beyond hope the other.

Adrenalin

It's best I put down my pen now.
I should give the trees
A deep watering,
I should hunt the undersides of leaves
For the snails
That have been eating the pansies,
I should butter a slice of bread,
I should keep everything low-keyed.

I sat down to write of adrenalin.
In the past month, two climbers
Lost their grip on El Capitan,
A parachutist
Pulled the wrong cord
Just before she hit a field of wheat,
Six bodies of rafters
Were wedged among rocks in the Kings River.

It was all for fun, see?
It was a way to take
A sluggish pond of blood
And make it race like the Kings.
I should put down my pen.
The trees have been dry too long,
The snails must be stopped,
And I keep seeing faces.

Imagination

for John Haines

So much of it has been given
To shaping deaths:
A hook between the shoulder blades,
The stake in the town square,
Guillotine and wicker basket,
A drum with a crank
To wind out the entrails,
Or now, free of our own history,
The imagination refined,
The lethal injection.

Always we picture
The martyr's eyes turned upward,
Dreaming another death,
One that only we deserve.
We want to drop
From rum and days of dancing
At the carnival in Rio.
Forget the causes: we want
To fade just as the lovely lady's
Yes fades in our ear.

But the dancer returns from Rio
To sell more insurance,
The yes strikes the anvil
In an ear that will live on
To gather no after no.
The end has no imagination;
It's likely to be a slight
Irritation to the ear,
Then a flare and fall of thought,
Like the striking of a match.

Against Dreaming

I cross the blue river
Of sleep
And kneel and drink from it.
This is safer than the well,
Which went bad weeks ago,
About the same time, in fact,
As the court ruled everything
I've done or wanted to do illegal.
Their officers have not followed me;
Clouds obliterate my spoor.
The only danger
Is falling into a dream
That might take an ugly turn.
To sleep but not to dream . . .
How can I keep it from me?
If I could have brought you here,
We could have played
Cards against dreaming,
Or that game
With your body I love,
Which is supremely illegal.
But there is no place
More solitary,
And I feel empty in my clothes,
As if, part by part,
Everything has been amputated.
This is how
The dream begins.

Night Game

I thought it was a beautiful game.
It was a game that I would rather
have played at night.

— Willy Mays

After a large hatch of moths,
We can watch the weaving
Of a doily
In front of each light standard,

And the grass
Takes on an almost eerie beauty;
It has never been a deeper green,
And the night has never been
A deeper night.

The hardwoods,
Worked so carefully on the lathes,
Shine their yellow, they are wands,
And the sound of broken magic,
The triple dying to a single,
Brings on a twinge of pain.

Twelfth inning:
The bad fans are all in their beds,
Dreaming microchips
Or pork belly futures,

And the last of us,
After the moves down, row by row,
To the box seats finally ours,
Dream
The unforgivable error,
The miraculous sacrifice.
Who cares what happens?

Why, we all do;
This is a matter of destiny,
Of fate in its rawest form,
It is a question of whether a man
Who throws knuckleballs
Merits divine grace or eternal scorn.

It's the sixteenth inning;
It is as if illness
Has been carried to an unbearable extreme.
There are going to be those who succumb,
And there will be those
Who take it in stride and live . . .

Thank the god of skill,
The sometimes more powerful god of luck,
It is all being decided in the dark,
Under the lights.

Disembarking

Everyone had a sly smile,
A little embarrassed,
A little guilty, even a bit silly,
Because almost everyone
Thought they were going to die--
Careening takeoff in a wind shear,
Collision midair,
Blown tires on landing,
Not to mention those terrorists
In every third seat--
And all through the flight
Regretted the stupidly undone,
The unsaid,
Mechanically ate the food
Disguised as food,
Watched the movie
No one had ever paid to see,
Listened to the attendants bowing
In schooled politeness,
Raised the shade to clouds
Parading, too near, as common clouds,
Carried on conversations
So empty they almost wished to die,
Clutched pillows stuffed
With kapok-of-comfort-lost,
Took the swaying piss of no comfort,
Flushed into the sucking wheeze,
Sat back down to no-smoking,
Seat-belt-required,
Ballooned in the whump of real earth at last,
Endured the high cicada-buzz

Of taxying,
Grabbed the carry-on
From the overhead bin,
And emerged, wide-eyed,
Terminal,
Faced with familiar faces,
The shy smile
Almost turning to a grin.

Mystery

The self is no mystery, the mystery is
That there is something for us to stand on.

                                   –George Oppen

There are no guardrails at Canyon de Chelly.
On the very edge
Of the great brow of rock,
I suffered a vertigo
That tied me forever to the earth.
I want to be here,
With the oak floors creaking under me,
And outside, among the flowers,
Where the columbine
Sensibly dies back upon itself
In the first freeze.
The mysteries are all here:
Roots, the leaves turning,
The spiders hard at their geometry lessons,
The seed that obeys perfectly
Its own limits,
The worms turning among the leaves,
Turning the leaves to compost,
Dung beetle and bottle fly,
The fluting of the white-crowned sparrow,
The shrill cries
Of the flickers, newly arrived,
The dog at his dreams,
The airiness of the dogwood,
The heaviness of the cork oak,
And the Bradford pear,
Burning its deepest reds like a candle flame,
And the sun, most mysterious,

Will be almost that red
Just before setting this evening.
The muddiness of the self
Can be forgiven, almost forgotten,
In the clarity of late October.

It Was for This

He carried the canoe through burdocks
And milkweed,
Across a pebbly plain,
And silently slipped onto the lake.
It was best when the water
Was black, bottomless,
And it was for this:
The broken moon falling,
The last bat leaving the stars
To fold itself into a shadow,
The island of rock barely seen,
Sleeping like a skull.
In an hour the heron
Would shake itself awake,
But for now,
Afloat between depths of water and sky,
He was himself,
Most solitary, without light,
Most alive.

Under Stars

It's night on the water in the canal,
Darker still in the kingfisher's burrow;
Night glistens among the day lilies,
Walking the track of a garden snail.

It's night in the red eye of a box turtle,
In the stirring of loam
Where a sprout splits the seed,
Night in the thought that is better off dead.

It's night in the doorway of my daughter's dream,
In the hand on my wife's shoulder;
Night stretches out in the shadow
Cast on the lawn by my shadow.

Night quietly searches for itself
Where the moon breaks up in a maple,
But without people under stars
There would be no one to find it.

Primitive Sand

How many years had the spring
Bubbled its silver into that tiny pond
At the stream's head?

On the bottom, the sand
Had boiled against itself so long
It was worn soft and slippery as talc.

I was just a boy,
With a boy's knees and a boy's head,
But I knew when I knelt

To drink there
How far that posture went back:
I could as well have been

An ape with my ass in the air.
When I rose,
I had the feeling I saw, dimly in shade,

One of the old ones,
The ones of the permanent frown,
Who forded a stream on sharp, primitive sand

To become us.
What a journey they made . . .
What a stream he crossed,

My dappled one, my beginning in time.
I pressed my hand flat against my brow
And then held the palm open toward him.

It was a salute I was sure I owed him,
Even if he couldn't read it,
Even if he wasn't there.

On the Road Home

In a valley of leafless scrub oaks
Greened by mistletoe,
A magpie
Hauls his long iridescent tail
Home through the dusk.
It has been a full day for him,
Scavenging at the roadside,
Yakking with friends.

I too had a full day:
A five-hour drive,
Yakking through lunch with friends,
Then reading poems for an hour.
It seemed to go well,
Though one, nervous,
Clearly upset about something else,
Perhaps a love grown too complex,
Nagged me for being simple.

The magpie builds its broad nest
Well hidden in mistletoe.
Even this most sociable of birds
Wants, at day's end,
Privacy, silence,
And I, less loquacious,
Secretly longed all day for this moment,
No car ahead of me,
No car in the mirror,
Just me, driving between hills
In the slanting shadows of evening,
Just me and this other
Simple bird.

Bear-Proof

for Jim Russell

There are those creatures
Who can't let a challenge die in the dark.
Muddy paw prints
On the front and top of the dumpster
Are so clear, so unsmeared by haste,
They look like a page in a police file;
His moves were cool and deliberate
As a safecracker's.
The locks, braided steel cables,
Bear-proof, so they said,
Broke cleanly when he threw back the lid.
What we thought we'd discarded for good--
All the trimmings and peels,
Every bottle and can--
Was tossed out onto the road in contempt.
I doubt his meal amounted to much,
But I don't think he cared what he took.
I think he hauled himself
Erect in the moonlight,
Looked upon what he'd done with a nod
And a single plumed huff of breath,
Then shuffled off,
Big-butted, complacent,
On his black trail between the pines.
He had a statement to make,
And, cleaning up after him,
His eloquence is as airily clear to me
As this mountain dawn:
Look, people, give it up, surrender;
I'm man-proof.

Egg

I'm scrambling an egg for my daughter.
"Why are you always whistling?" she asks.
"Because I'm happy."
And it's true,
Though it stuns me to say it aloud;
There was a time when I wouldn't
Have seen it as my future.
It's partly a matter
Of who is there to eat the egg:
The self fallen out of love with itself
Through the tedium of familiarity,
Or this little self,
So curious, so hungry,
Who emerged from the woman I love,
A woman who loves me in a way
I've come to think I deserve,
Now that it arrives from outside me.
Everything changes, we're told,
And now the changes are everywhere:
The house with its morning light
That fills me like a revelation,
The yard with its trees
That cast a bit more shade each summer,
The love of a woman
That both is and isn't confounding,
And the love
Of this clamor of questions at my waist.
Clamor of questions,
You clamor of answers,
Here's your egg.

Family Man

2:00 A.M.: if I don't make my move now,
My bladder's a goner.
Hazily I lift the seat,
Relieve myself in a rectangle of moonlight,
And hazily lower the seat again:
One must learn to do this without thinking
To live at peace among women.

In the hallway between the two bedrooms,
I pause a moment to listen.
I'm at the exact center of two breathings,
Wife and daughter,
The four lovely lungs of my life,
Winds from the north and south that meet to fan
All my earthly fires.

Smoke

for Dianne

There are too many things to do in life,
So our daughter's always doing two at once
And pays the price in pain.
Looking backward while running forward
She bangs her head on the edge of an open door,
Eating while talking
She bites her tongue and yelps;
She feels she didn't deserve it:
The monologue was going so well.
"One thing at a time," we say,
But it's impossible.

Focus comes with age.
We are old enough to think of one thing
All day long,
And that has its own price.
For weeks you've thought of death,
Collapsing like a star,
Growing denser and denser inside your father,
Absorbing a bit more of his light each day,
And your own darkness has been broken
Only in millisecond white bursts.

One thing at a time . . .
It will get darker yet,
And then the milliseconds will expand
Into a universe of hours,
Perhaps uninterrupted days, with luck a month . . .
One thing at a time,
But by the time that we implode
Into our own black cores,

And the edges of us become wisps of smoke
Drifting across the Sierra's ridge,
We will have been many things:

Children,
Less sure than some,
But strong enough to have risen
From the ashes of our parents' deaths;
Parents,
And, despite our advice that couldn't be taken,
Good ones, I think;
Lovers,
Through light, through dark, into smoke,
And good ones, I know.

Cobalt

He leadeth me beside the still waters . . .
I remember that,
So many times, him holding the minnow bucket,
Leading me down the dock
To a boat whose prow lifted and sank
In the wake
From some idiot water skier.
Sputter of motor,
Blue oil slick--
I don't know a more beautiful blue--
Deepest cobalt, spreading in our own small wake.
Drifting in lily pads,
We took northern pike, crappie,
Inedible dogfish,
Hated perch, always small and too bony
And full of worms, they said,
Whatever came our way,
Still bobbing among the power boats.

Then the lake's surface
Went from yellow to tangerine
To a lucky penny,
And we were alone there,
Ringed by a stillness of black trees.
I'd like to tell you
We opened out of ourselves
And talked,
But, as I try to bring it back,
I see us losing
Each other's faces in silence,

But in a silence that was not a loss.
We were best at saying
Nothing, lost in a quietude
Pure as cobalt.
Sometimes the motor wasn't started again:
The fish on their stringer,
Moon-mouthed,
Bumping the side of the boat,
Perch and dogfish
To be buried in the garden,
To feed roots white as their flesh,
Pike and crappie
For the table,
His hands, my hands,
Then both of us pulling our hands
To his chest, my chest,
His chest,
Under the opening stars.

Reader

It's been six months since we talked.
Chalk it up to my laziness,
Which at times I take as my birthright,
And partly to the necessity,
Once in a while,
To shut down, be silent, and live,
Just live.

That has everything to do with my birthright;
My father never just lived,
He even had to work at his vision of laziness,
His cabin on Lake Frances,
The lock closed on his dream,
Which became something to repaint,
And replumb, and always,
Always, redream,
Redream to a level of satisfaction,
And in our family,
No one has ever been satisfied.

Maybe I haven't talked to you,
Reader,
Because I've been tinkering with locks
Without satisfaction,
Nothing opened.

But on a night not long ago,
I wandered into my daughter's bedroom.
Officially, I was there
To say good night and get my kiss.
Unofficially, I saw her before she saw me,
Reading there,

Book on the pillow,
Rapt, quilted,
Reading the way we all read
When the words are our own and beyond us
And, therefore, exactly ours.

I thought of us, then, reader,
Reading about people we will never know,
But reading, in good faith,
Because we want to know ourselves, exactly,
In another.

And I knew her, then, exactly,
Exactly as myself,
A different book, but the same age,
The book against the pillow
At almost the same angle of vision,
And surely the same cells,
The blood of my blood reading,
The soft cone of lamplight,
The corners too shadowed for a child,
But eased by the lamplight,
The book propped against the pillow,
The little lady reading,
Full of herself and the book,
Dear reader,
Herself and someone's book.

This Life

Look, I'm not going
To come back as a saint, or even a gopher
Burrowing your lawn,
And I'm not going to live on and on and on,
Bored, finally, I'd guess,
In sweet, saintly air.
I'm going to rot
Quickly as an orange in mulch.
At this moment, I don't want to mourn
The matter of fact.
As a matter of fact, my life
Keeps edging its way
Closer to me,
And it moves closest
When I plant a white birch, or an azalea,
Or take a slow breath close to the hair
Of the woman I love.
The birch may or may not outlive me.
The azalea likely won't.
I don't know
What's best for my wife.
These, though important, are small questions.
I pass carbon dioxide to the trees,
The azaleas; they throw
A little oxygen my way,
I throw a little love my wife's way.
Generosity seizes her;
What I've given comes back threefold.
These exchanges
Are as simple and familiar

As pollination.
If you want to say
This life
Is nothing, this life I inhale,
This life as sweet
To me as the air passing across a citrus blossom,
If you want to say this life
Is merely the bridge
To the life we're asked to dream of,
You are my enemy.
I'm afraid I've offended you.
Look, I think I see
What you see,
And I won't deny the power
Of that wispy edge, horizon to horizon,
Of a cloud
Never to be scattered by wind.
You have forever;
I'm not sure there's time to explain.
Let me put it this way:
It has always been a fault of mine
To take things too personally;
You're not my enemy,
But you may have to answer
To this life.

CZECHOSLOVAKIA

Cemetery in Dolni Dobrouc, Czechoslovakia

Over the stone wall, an old man
Cuts hay with a scythe, stacks it
With a wooden rake.

A diamond in the dark
Is poor as this old villager,
But birches shivering in the sun of Bohemia

Are pure silver.
Rodina Hanzlikova.
Family Hanzlicek.

My people,
Ashes;
The unburned shards of bone

Are diamonds in the heavy loam,
Unlit beneath geraniums.
The old man's work is done.

The logs of his cottage
Were hewn two hundred years ago
By people whose names are still spoken.

He will lie back against his wall,
Sigh and take the sun,
Drink an amber glass of cool beer.

Rodina Hanzlikova.
No given names; there could be two
Or twenty turned into the soil.

My work is done.
I will return to my forty-year-old house,
In a country where

No one can pronounce my name,
But I was here a while,
Silent in the sun shivering the birches,

Among my people,
Nameless,
Ashes.

Janacek

On October 1, 1905, the composer, Leos Janacek, was having a miserable day. He stood on Charles Bridge, looking at the bronze figure of a martyr who was not fully martyred yet, since he was still being tortured. In his briefcase, Janacek had a score that had just been rejected, no doubt not for the first time. He took out the score, showed it to the near-martyr with a scowl, as if to suggest that a lesser pain is still pain, and torture, after all, is torture, and then he cast what was more than bread to him upon the waters of the Vltava. A wind flowing downriver scattered the pages. He later told a friend, rather pleasantly, that the sheets of his music had floated on the river like white swans. In Janacek's day, swans on the Vltava were not a common sight; now they are everywhere on the river. On October 1, 1905, Leos Janacek would never have dreamed that his reputation and the swan population of Prague would grow in perfect synchrony. This is understandable; no matter how beautiful swans might be, they are not very musical.

Prague, Late November, 1989

One quarter of a million people are gathered on the square. After seven hundred lost battles for Czech freedom, they can feel in the air that the time may have come to win one. They light candles at the base of the statue of Wenceslas on horseback; candles, like ardor, burn even in this cold. The tricolor, which must only be flown side by side with the Soviet flag, waves all across the square in sudden solitary dignity. When Alexander Dubcek appears on a balcony and throws out his arms in an embrace that enfolds an entire nation, a giddiness rises among them, as if they are breathing laughing gas. They chant, "Jakes to the garbage, Jakes to the garbage," and then, "Dubcek to the Castle, Dubcek to the Castle." The Party twitches, but it is dead. Privilege is dead. The professor who has been stoking boilers on the night shift for twenty years may teach again. A man who closed down his newspaper in '68 is passing out free copies of today's revived edition. A voice over a loudspeaker calls for attention, and the crowd instantly falls silent. There is an urgent message: a nine-year-old boy named Honza has become separated from his mother. "Be brave, Honza, be brave," they chant. No Czech can be truly free until Honza finds his mama.

Prague Wreaths

You never have to walk far
To find a silver foil
Wreath with its marker,
Yet they always come as a shock:
Against a wall
Beside the gentle sweep of the Vltava,
Near an apartment entrance
On a busy street
(There must have been a hundred witnesses),
Over the buttons to a freight elevator
In a department store.
All about the city,
Men forced to find a way
To be more than men
Were executed on the spot
By Germans.

I can hardly imagine myself
In that place.
Maybe I'm talking,
Maybe a book lies open on the table,
Maybe my hands
Move beneath an eiderdown
To map a body,
And in an instant the thought,
The word, the caress,
Whatever the search,
Is halted
By a gunshot in the street . . .

In front of a wreath at the gate
To my favorite park,

A blue titmouse
Couldn't care less which fool
Inspires my politics.
It's morning, he woke hungry,
So he flits down from a maple
To eat the crumbs of a breakfast roll
From my open hand.
Forty years ago,
Some hungrier distant relative of his
Saw the fall, the blood,
Right here,
Of Karel Zbiral (1897-1945),
A creature
Who could not be tamed.

MAHLER

Mahler 1

Neither ought he by any means to be called unhappy, for he who had been given so rich a substance, so warm a heart, and so eloquent a tongue, cannot be classified among either the happy or the unhappy. He knew of fervent exaltation and of bitter sorrow, and so strong an inward agitation is a finer gift of the gods than mere happiness.

–Bruno Walter

The photos of you conducting, in tails,
Make you look like a fly
Climbing a window.
Just so:
I'll bet the orchestra was a window,
A surface that would reveal
Your heart
Or be shattered by your scowl.
Gustav, I grew up in factories, oiled beyond
The gracious, free, coarse soap at the circular sinks.
I grew up thinking "Yes, We Have No Bananas"
Was music,
So there was much I had to leave behind
To arrive at another music,
A music I had to discover like a foreign country.
I got held up at customs--
"What is this you've been listening to?"--
But their pitying
Headshakes set me free at last.
When I put down my bags and first felt
Your strings wash over me,
A window opened.
It was suddenly all right
To be the ignorant prince of emotions I felt

But would never understand.
Understanding was beside the point.
I was neither happy nor unhappy;
I was moved,
And that was good soap,
That got well below my skin.
My students want novels with happy endings,
But my conscience gives them pain on pain.
We are whole or we are nothing;
There is a side of us we know and like
And want more of
Because it is so easily known,
Familiar as a birthmark,
But the other side,
The side that leaves us lost in love
Or something more vague,
A plain deep ache,
The side you taught me not to fear,
Is both cloud and clarity
And may even be more truly what we are:
Unhappy, happy selves.

Mahler 2

So closely bound up is the act of creation in me with all my experience that when my mind and spirit are at rest I can compose nothing.

–Mahler

The berries on the privets are ripe,
And the annual aerial invasion
Of cedar waxwings has begun.
They circle, call "see-ee-ee" to each other,
Then settle in to gorge.
They shit purple so fast it sounds
Like rain on the leaves.
This is a creature built around hunger;
Even their eyes slant
In a vicious leer of appetite.
"Happy as a lark," we say,
Because we've never seen one eat,
But the face at the height of ecstasy
Can wear the look of pain,
And even pain, at least, has depth
And carries us somewhere.
Some of us these days
Can no longer find anyone to listen
To where we've been,
So we pay good money
To professional listeners
To have our minds made well,
Only to suffer loss of appetite
And find ourselves carried
Neither high nor deep.
Our guilts and fears and hungers
Are hard-earned;
We should wear them

Like the waxwing wears its crown.
You were propelled
From note to note
By the blind force
Of simply living a life.
You may have ended some days
With a well-drawn map of hell,
But at least it was clearly drawn,
And we who read it now
Know exactly where you dared to go.
You take us down without mercy
To where the only music
Might as well be bone against bone,
The fire in the cave gone out,
The wall paintings of the things
We loved extinguished too,
But you never abandon us there.
It's your nature to burst
From the mouth of the night and soar,
Singing, "See-ee-ee, see-ee-ee,"
Hungry as the wind,
Happy in the way of waxwings.

Mahler 3

Last night's sky was moonless.
The stars, as usual,
Were aging gracefully.
The problem with my aging is
I don't have a friend
Who isn't aging with me.
One by one, like evening stars
Of evil omen,
The afflictions emerge.
The last has come too near,
And it's dragging me
Down, down.
My oldest friends,
A couple married since their teens,
Called to tell me she is ill.
We've always been noisy with each other--
The raucousness of crows
Sharing a hatred or a love
From our singular tree--
But last night we spoke
Almost in whispers.
Gustav, here's the problem:
Our fate is a melody
That's been humming in our heads
Since we took on the habit
Of occasional thought,
But it has been the bass line,
Barely audible.
Now strings and reeds and horns
Join in, and the melody
Surrounds us like the night,

Undeniable.
It isn't darkness, though,
That sets the tone;
It is our passion for each other,
The sense that our lives
Have gone on in all the parallels
Affection lays out for us.
So many of your symphonies
Abandon the bass line for the ascent
Of a finale that is no finale,
Since its echoes cancel silence.
That's the strength we must take from you,
So that the parallels run on,
So that the echoes re-echo,
So that fate retreats to its dark corner
For further thought,
So that nothing happens,
Not now, not yet,
Not under this sky.

Mahler 4

You penned your songs for the death of children;
I have this one
In another language.
It was a night below freezing,
And someone thought they could heat
Their mobile home with the kitchen stove:
Four kids are gone, just gone,
By fire,
Wisps, an awful word,
This way.
They give us the news at night,
So that too often we go to bed
Head down,
As if to a ritual of the dark.
We try not to be that dark;
We try not to be what we suffer.
What would we be
Without the power of the wings
Of sex to lighten and carry us--
O and O upon our lips--
Beyond all we've seen and heard?
Children die,
All our childhoods die;
Only the body of another
Takes the gravity from our bodies.
You often sang those songs, too,
From allegro to adagio;
It was a matter of mood, of weight,

Of the gravity of the night.
Sometimes the O must be shaped
By tragedy,
But sometimes, like a gift
From the gods,
There is the good O,
The O ecstatic.

Mahler 5

Lose a limb, then you can cry,
Once.
That's the way we raise our boys;
There shall be no weeping
In the house of our Lord.
That is why our men
Can never break down with any dignity.
A death comes near--
Their own or that of someone near--
And the cry, yowl or whimper,
Is that of a boy.
But, Gustav, you came from Bohemia.
When you blubbered
Between Alma's breasts,
That most earthy woman held out
An angelic prow to your quivering lips,
Your whimper was seraphic,
And what came out was an adagio
That again and again
Has moved the world to tears,
And I don't mean tears to
Mama, Mama.
I don't doubt what lured
Your nose to Alma's scent;
It was self-pity sure enough,
But it was as if you'd lost a limb.
Dignity is not a matter of what enters
The spirit to make us cry,
It's what comes out when we do.
The spirit can be molded
To something as small and hard-cased

As a walnut,
Or it can open out like an oriental fan,
Displaying all its colors.
When you opened,
The whole inner landscape
Was spread before us,
And now there is the music,
Fanning, fanning,
With no hint of coolness,
All ardor and heat
And dignity,
A good cry.

Mahler 6

*Any type of lyricism when face to face with death . . . is superfluous, an
impertinence even. Death is death. It doesn't have any adjectives.*

–Miroslav Holub

"The time between
When the gas struck his face
And when he stopped
Breathing was thirteen minutes.
He was unconscious for
One minute."
So said the mouthpiece
Of the executioner
Of the state of Mississippi,
Bare of any adjectives.
Twelve minutes
Before the light shrank to nothing!
Did you have any idea it took that long?
Nor did I,
But it's with me now as one fact
In a catalog of facts
I'd rather not know.
I also cannot help but catalog
Things I've done in segments of time
No longer than those twelve minutes:
Fell in love with my wife,
Took marriage vows
On a hill above Watts Valley Road,
Signed papers to buy a house,
Buried my father,
Conceived a child . . .
You get my drift, Maestro.

Much can be done in twelve minutes
Unless you are strapped in a chair
With a stethoscope taped to your chest.
In that circumstance your mind
Probably doesn't leaf through
The pages of your past one by one;
It must suddenly fill with trivia,
The details of your own humiliation--
How convulsions pulling at your face
Will appear to the witnesses,
Whether you'll mess your pants
In spite of the precautions
Of forgoing the last meal
And two hours before dawn on the toilet,
Whether some paroxysm will provoke
An involuntary cry
That will echo against
The walls of the chamber . . .
That sort of thing.
When we can't tell
The torturer from the tortured,
When death
Is twelve minutes of terror,
When it rises like one of your melodies
And takes flight from all its adjectives,
We think it's Biblical.

Mahler 7

A writer needs ancestors. He must know some of them by name. When he thinks he is going to choke on his own name, which he cannot get rid of, he harks back to ancestors, who bear happy, deathless names of their own. They may smile at his importunity, but they do not rebuff him. They too need others, in their case descendants.

–Elias Canetti

Smile at my importunity,
But once again the moon has pared itself thin,
And I'm tired of talking to my hands.
So, ancestor,
Leave the realm of roots,
Lick the ashes from your lips,
And sit beside me for another talk;
Your descendant needs you,
Gustav,
To lift this heaviness.
Float along, float along,
Feel a downward tug,
Pray for feathers,
And they hand you a rock, right?
My doctor, a wise man
Who also loves music, says:
"If you continue to feel this way about things
You can't control--
And you probably should--
Your blood pressure will continue to rise."
Simple as that: we incinerate from within,
Or what's in the mirror
Bores us.
It's wrong to think there's a choice, though.
It's all those ancestral Bohunks--
You know the type; you were there.
For a thousand years, popes and monarchs

Dressed out their hopes like deer;
Of course the spirit took on a heaviness,
A gravity at the core,
When all seemed upside down,
As if they looked at the world
Hanging by the ankles from a plane tree.
Benes and Masaryk cut them down,
The lightness came at last,
They danced a while in the clearing,
Then became a gift to the Russians.
My grandfather
Stropped his straightedge at the kitchen sink
Under a calendar of scenes from Prague.
"Tell me about Bohemia," I said,
"Tell me where we came from."
His fingers just below his ear
Pulled the skin of his cheek taut,
The razor rasped,
And in the mirror I saw the shine
Go out of his eyes.
The heaviness descended in the warm room
Like fog.
He told me nothing
Because he had to save himself from sadness,
But he passed on the sadness anyway,
To my father and me,
Both of us moody men.
Thanks for listening, Gustav.
Now let us listen to something of yours.
Maybe it will change the mood
Of this night,
But I have my doubts.

Mahler 8

There are times you get so far
Down into pain
I think you'll never rise.
Where does the light come from?
Twenty horns blat fear
Up and down the spine;
The flesh becomes an eerie,
Eely thing--O, let me out!
The strings wring the heart.
When I was a boy,
I kept captured pets--
A tree frog, snakes, a shrew--
Things I didn't know how to feed.
The tree frog withered
To a dime-sized wafer;
They all starved and stank
Until I learned at last:
Leave the wild alone.
I think it's fair
That they don't leave me alone,
That I feel I have to tell you
Their story.
We shouldn't get by with murders,
Even ones we cause
Before we learn
The little we'll know of mercy,
Before we learn
Pain.
Some just don't feel it,
But those who do
Know there is no ladder out of it.
We must sometimes

Sit with it at night
Like people sit with the dying,
But it may not die;
It may not be ready to leave us alone;
We may not have earned light yet.
All right, Gustav,
Give me this night
My nightly pain.
I will sit with you;
We will not rise.

Mahler 9

From time to time, as is the way
With children,
I was bad news to my father.
Sweet as his own father,
He tried to hide it,
But even I could read his face.
He thought of things I'd do,
And I didn't,
And then, by the time I'd done
A thing or two,
He'd died
And gone off on his travels.
Maestro,
You didn't live to see it,
Streptococcus saw to that,
My grandfather didn't live to see it,
An embolism saw to that,
My father had another place to go
After his heart abandoned him,
But now, in early December, 1989,
I have lived to see
The Czechs cry, "*Svobodu, Svobodu,*"
"Freedom, Freedom,"
And maybe, at long last,
They will have some,
And that is good news,
But all three of you missed it,
And my father left
Even before he could be a grandfather.
What lightness

My daughter would have brought him . . .
He has been a traveler for so long,
He must, by now,'
Be at the very fringes of the universe.
In the final movement of your Ninth,
The melody keeps getting thinner and thinner,
Played by fewer and fewer instruments,
Slowed, slowed again,
Until it is held only by a few strings,
Almost silence itself,
And then it just floats off
Like a quiet death.
And that is how I imagine my father,
Floating through space
Like a melody above the orchestra's body,
Between one bare
Wisp of light and another,
Searching,
As he did in life,
But he must come here,
To earth,
For an end to bad news,
And I don't think he can make it
So far back.